# EXPLORE

# TROWBRIDGE

## John Collingwood and Emma Worth

This book belongs to

.................................................................

*I'm happy to share but please take care!*

Trowbridge

# Welcome

So here we are in Trowbridge, county town of Wiltshire, where a modern shopping centre sits comfortably on the site of an ancient castle. Below are four images, which will help you navigate your way through the pages and through your town. You can check out the meanings of the words in **bold** in the glossary on page 31.

**Find Francis!** See if you can spot the ghostly image of Francis Frith - famous Victorian photographer - lurking in the shadows of his photographs!

Now please step this way . . .

**Check it out!**
Things to see and do

This Way!

Look out for these symbols in the book:

**Think about it!**
Interact with history

**Gore of Yore**
Gruesome doings of yesteryear

**Did You Know?**
Fascinating facts

The rainbow colour band on the timeline is to help you with dates. It starts with red for the Stone Age and ends with violet for today. So you'll be able to see at a glance the period of time each page refers to.

**TIMELINE**

*A guide through the ages*

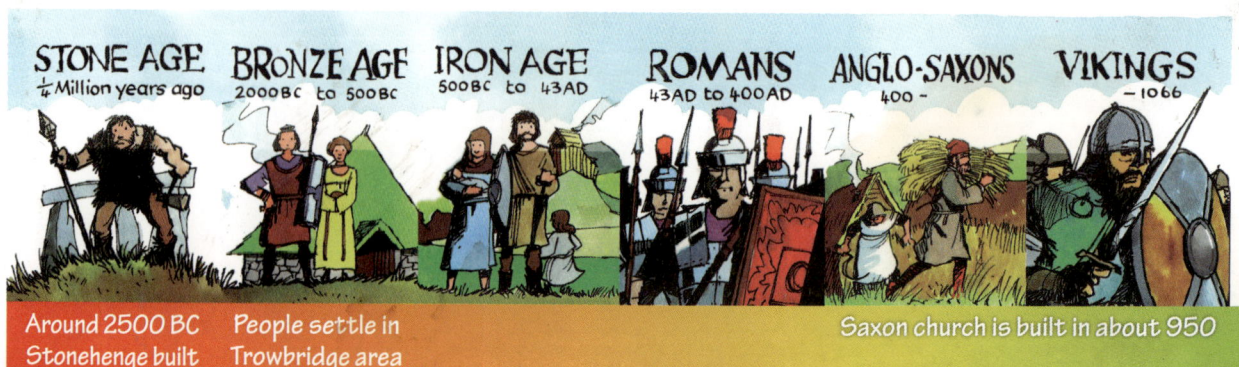

| STONE AGE | BRONZE AGE | IRON AGE | ROMANS | ANGLO-SAXONS | VIKINGS |
|---|---|---|---|---|---|
| ¼ Million years ago | 2000BC to 500BC | 500BC to 43AD | 43AD to 400AD | 400 – | – 1066 |

Around 2500 BC Stonehenge built

People settle in Trowbridge area

Saxon church is built in about 950

# EXPLORE TROWBRIDGE

## CONTENTS

**NORMANS** Middle Ages 1066 –

**MIDDLE AGES** –1485

**TUDORS** 1485 – 1603

**STUARTS** 1603 – 1714

**GEORGIANS** 1714 – 1837

**VICTORIANS** 1837 – 1901

**MODERN TIMES** 1901 —

King Stephen lays siege to Trowbridge castle

First Church of St James built in 1450

John Aubrey writes that Trowbridge is a "great clothing town" in 1685

Thomas Helliker hanged in 1803

Isaac Pitman introduces shorthand in 1837

Shires shopping centre opens in 1990

**BRONZE AGE**
2000 B.C. to 500 B.C.

# IN THE BEGINNING

People began to settle in the Trowbridge area long before the birth of Christ. We know this because during excavations in the town centre in 1977 and 1986-88, pottery was discovered together with tools made from flint and animal bones. These are believed to date back to the **Bronze Age** ( 2000 BC – 500 BC). Archaeologists also found pottery and coins that suggest people continued to live here during the Roman era (AD43 – AD400).

The settlement developed on a low ridge alongside the River Biss, which runs through the centre of the town today. The river also probably helped give Trowbridge its name. The name Trowbridge actually comes from a Saxon word "treowbrycg" meaning "Tree Bridge". So the first permanent settlement may have grown up where a track used by travellers reached a wooden bridge across the Biss – possibly near to the entrance of the ASDA store today.

*Above: Asda at "treowbrycg"*

*Right: A view of the River Biss from "treowbrycg"*

*Below: An artist's impression of Saxon Houses*

During the Saxon period (AD400 – 1066) this small farming community grew slowly. The foundations of a stone Saxon church have been found on the site of the present Trowbridge museum. By this time the settlement was part of the land of a Saxon lord. This lord at the time of the Domesday Book (1086) was called Brictric, whose father before him had owned it at the time of the Norman Conquest (1066).

Why do you think so many towns have their origins at places where rivers could be crossed? What advantages would such spots have had in early times?

Trowbridge is called "Straburg" in the Domesday Book. Various other names for the town have also existed over time such as "Thoroughbridge" and "Trolbridge".

It was after the Norman Conquest that Trowbridge began to grow in importance with the building of a castle.

The Romans had to withdraw their army from Britain in the 5th century AD because their huge eastern border in Europe was under attack from the so called "Barbarian" tribes.

Go to www.domesdaybook.co.uk and find out:

**This Way!**

1. Why is the Domesday Book so called?

2. How long did it take to write?

3. What was the book made out of?

After the Norman Conquest, King William I wanted to know much more about the England he had conquered. How many people inhabited each area? Who lived in a castle and who lived in a cottage? Did they own vast estates or a couple of pigs? Most important, how much tax could they pay to support his army?! All this information was written down in the Domesday Book.

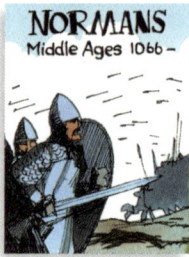

# CASTLES AND CRIMES

After William, Duke of Normandy, beat King Harold at the Battle of Hastings, the Conqueror rewarded his supporters by giving them English land. The Trowbridge area passed to Edward of Salisbury who, in turn, passed it to Humphrey de Bohun when he married Edward's daughter Maud - a large wedding present!

We don't know exactly when the castle was built. However, we do know that King Stephen laid **siege** to it in 1139 during the **civil war** between King Stephen and his cousin Matilda. These cousins both thought they were the rightful heir to the English throne! The fact that the siege failed shows that the castle's defences must have been strong.

### PARLEZ-VOUS FRANÇAIS?

The building of the castle would have had a big impact on the lives of local people. Some may have had to give up their homes to make way for it. How would the local people have felt about that? Remember too, that the Normans spoke French and brought new laws and customs. How would they have treated the local Saxons?

The earliest castle was almost certainly of the Norman motte and bailey design. You can't see any remains of it today, but the curved line from the town bridge up Wicker Hill and Fore Street follows the original path of the outer wall and ditch. The name Wicker Hill comes from the wickerwork or wooden hurdles, which formed part of the outer defences. The main part of the castle stood on the site that is now The Shires shopping centre.

*Wicker Hill in about 1955*

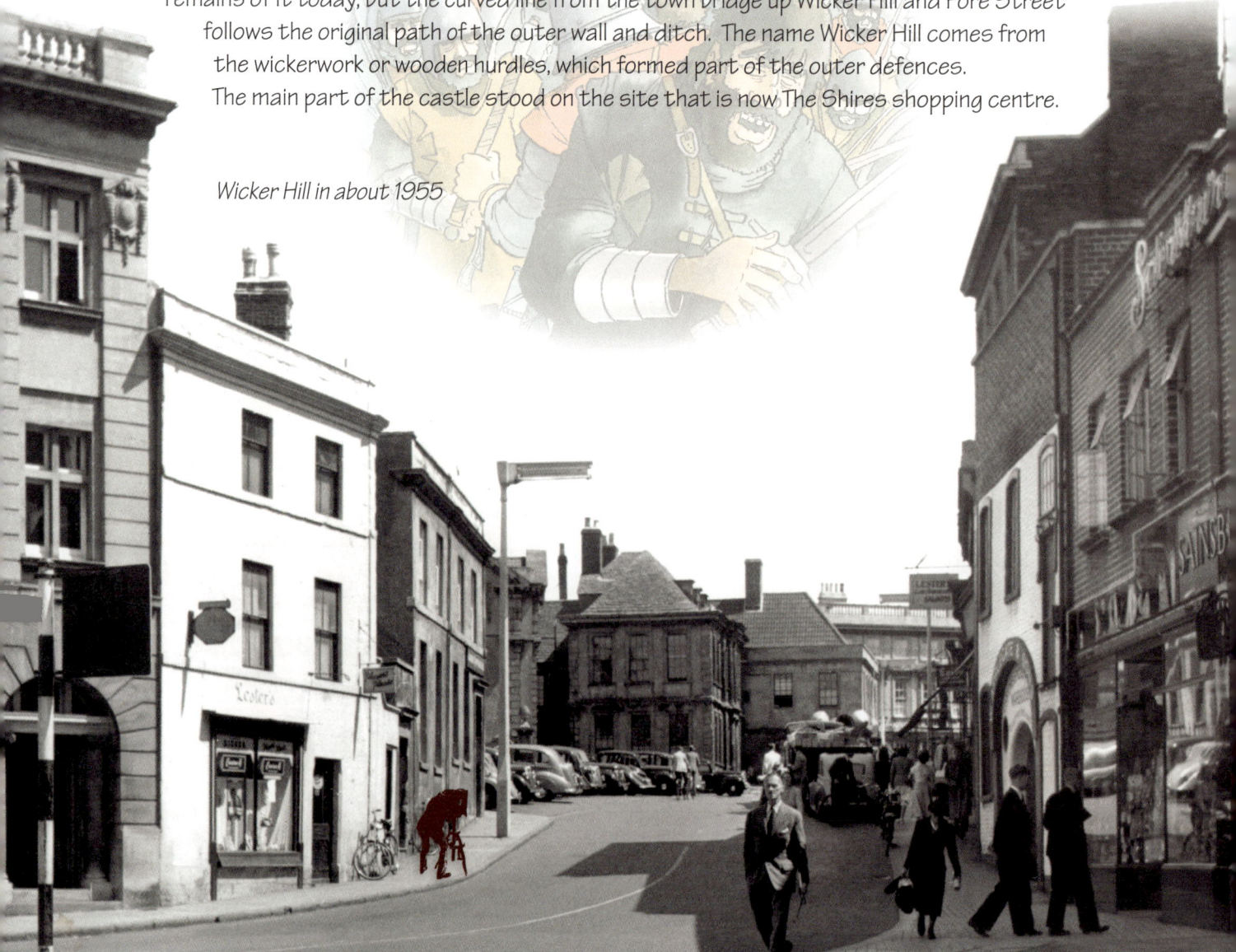

- Castles were **medieval** military bases. William wanted to make sure he kept control of England. Soldiers based in the castle could be sent to any nearby area where the Saxons were showing signs of resistance.

- The motte of Trowbridge castle was so steep that if someone got drunk and rolled down it he would probably die.

- Archaeologists found evidence that tells us the inhabitants of the castle were healthy: their diet included hazelnuts, blackberries, strawberries, apples and pears. Bones of cattle, sheep, pigs and hare were discovered in the cesspits. That's where sewage was disposed of!

## A MOTTE AND BAILEY CASTLE

## MOTTE AND BAILEY WORDMATCH

Match the words below with their corresponding place on the Motte and Bailey drawing.
Write your answers in the spaces provided.

**BAILEY
GATEWAY
MOTTE
WOODEN KEEP
MOAT
PALLISADE**

Answers on page 32

This Way!

1.
2.
3.
4.
5.
6.

Go and visit Farleigh Hungerford Castle, which is just 3 miles outside Trowbridge. This was a medieval castle built in the 14th century by Thomas Hungerford. Find out which member of the Hungerford family imprisoned his wife here for 4 years and was then beheaded by Henry VIII for treason and witchcraft.

This Way!

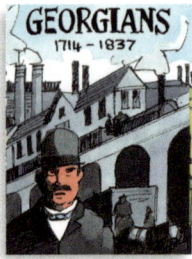

# BOOM TIME FOR THE

The making of woollen cloth was the biggest industry in England for 600 years - from the 12th to the 18th century. In the 1720s, the famous writer, Daniel Defoe, travelled through Great Britain and produced a guide-book. He was obviously impressed by the high quality of the cloth made in Trowbridge as he records that it was worn "in England by the better sort of people".

Most of the people living in Trowbridge would have been involved in the production of woollen cloth. The **clothiers** controlled this production from the time they bought the raw wool until they sold the finished cloth. The processes for making cloth were carried out in the clothiers' and workers' own homes. Here the wool was:

- *carded* - straightened and cleaned
- *spun* - drawn out and twisted into a long thread
- *woven* – made into a fabric by interlacing on a loom

The streets of Trowbridge would have echoed with the whirring of spinning wheels and the clanking of looms. Only the fulling stage - where the cloth was made heavier through shrinking and beating - took place at the clothier's mill.

After fulling, the cloth was stretched and dried on tenter racks. This is where we get the saying, "on tenter hooks", which means we are feeling in suspense.

## Parade of wealth

The clothiers became very rich. You can see this from the kind of houses they had built. Number 64 Fore Street, which is now Lloyds Bank, is still grand and imposing. The Parade boasted the finest clothiers' houses in Wiltshire.

Compare the photo of the Parade in 1900 with how it looked in 1965. There are horse-droppings in the first image and no cars. Then see how the Parade looks today.

This Way!

The Parade in 1900

The Parade in 1965

The Parade in 2006

# WOOLLEN INDUSTRY

These fine houses in The Parade might give the impression that Trowbridge in the early 18th century was a desirable place to live. However, this was far from true.

- Some of our surnames today are connected with the cloth industry – Shepherd, Lamb, Taylor, Weaver, Dyer, Webster, Tucker and Fuller.

- An unmarried lady is sometimes called a *spinster*. Originally, a spinster was a woman who earned her living through spinning.

An open sewer ran down Fore Street and another called Sluts Brook or S**ts Brook ran down Back Street.

Townsfolk emptied their **chamber pots** and made dunghills in the street.

Butchers slaughtered animals in the street and left the offal lying about.

Pigs roamed the streets.

It's hard for us to understand how people put up with this. Remember there were no local councils at that time to organise waste disposal.

Fore Street in 1900

# THE FACTORY AGE

The 18th century was a time of great inventions and change. In the woollen cloth industry, new machines such as the Spinning Jenny and the Flying Shuttle meant that yarn could be spun and woven at much greater speed.

**Join the dots to draw a Spinning Jenny.**

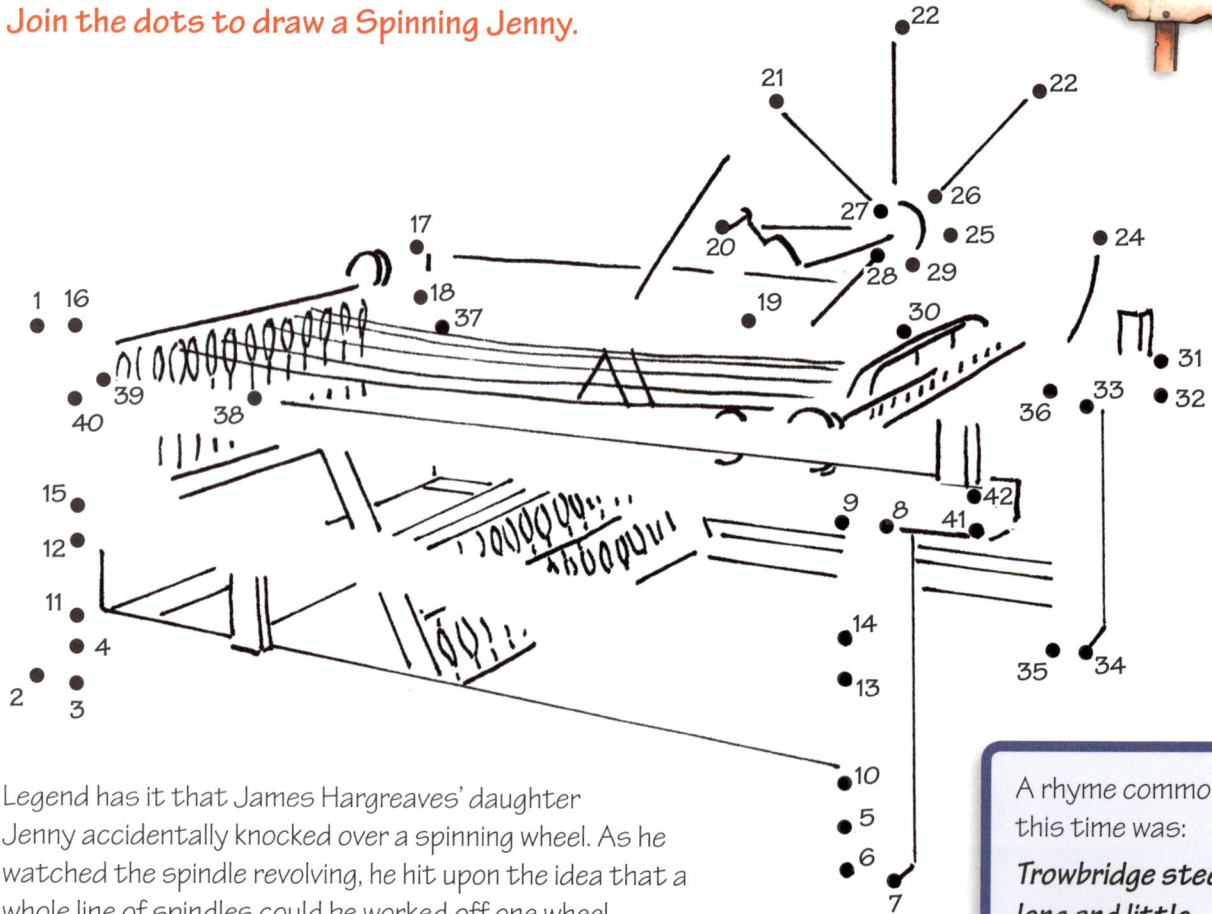

This Way!

Legend has it that James Hargreaves' daughter Jenny accidentally knocked over a spinning wheel. As he watched the spindle revolving, he hit upon the idea that a whole line of spindles could be worked off one wheel.

A rhyme common at this time was:

*Trowbridge steeple long and little Narrow streets and dirty people.*

In this photo you can see Ashton Mill as it looked in 1923. The 38-metre-high octagonal chimney was demolished to make way for the relief road.

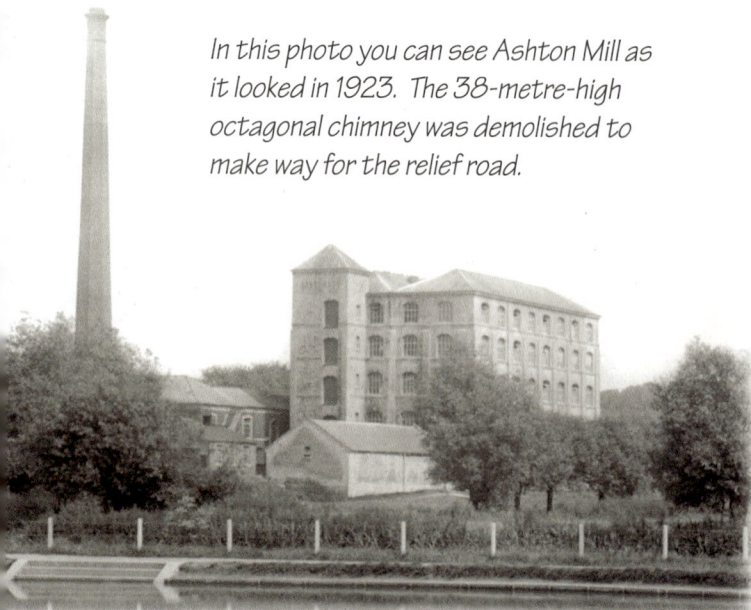

## All change

However, the biggest change in Trowbridge was a result of steam power. To make steam you need coal; in the dawn of the 19th century a canal was built, which connected Trowbridge to Radstock, where there were coal mines. The first factory in Trowbridge built to use steam was Bridge Mill near the Town Bridge.

The factories completely changed Trowbridge. These five-storey buildings were the largest most people had ever seen. There were no laws against polluting the environment and the high chimneys poured out filthy smoke.

This Way!

Visit Trowbridge Museum where you can see some examples of early spinning and weaving machines.

*A Spinning Jenny at Trowbridge Museum*

The factories also changed the lives of the **inhabitants** of Trowbridge. Most no longer worked at home, but instead had to get up before dawn and toil in a noisy factory until darkness fell. One exception was the weavers. They continued to work in their cottages until the 1860s, when weaving sheds were added to the spinning mills.

Studley Mill still stands but it is no longer a busy factory.

Find out what it is used for today.

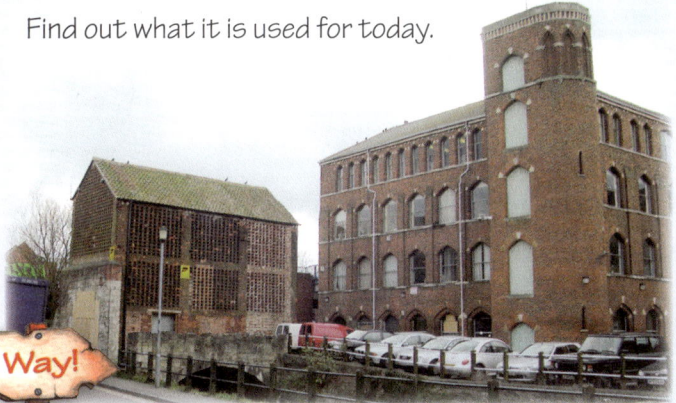

This Way!

- The change from producing things by hand to production by machines was called the Industrial Revolution.
- Britain was the first country in the world where this happened. From the late 1700s to the mid 1800s Britain was the richest nation in the world.
- The first ever factory was built by Richard Arkwright in Cromford, Derbyshire in 1771.
- Before steam, machines were powered by water or horses.
- Even when factories used steam power and no longer needed to be located by rivers, they were often called mills.

This photo of a terrace of weavers' cottages in Castle Street was taken in 1955. As you see from the modern photo, the cottages still stand. Notice the long windows in the top floor. The looms were positioned close by so that the weavers could see to do their work. There were no electric lights in those days!

# HARDSHIP IN THE FACTORIES

Although the **economy** in Trowbridge grew as a result of the **mass-production** of woollen cloth and many people became rich - particularly the factory owners - for many life was harsh. The greatest scandal of the 'factory age' was the employment of children, which, by today's standards, was cruelty.

Children as young as 7 laboured from 6 in the morning until 8 in the evening, sometimes without a break to eat. The hours could be even longer, but they were not paid overtime. Often they had to walk long distances to the factories without shoes, as they could not afford them. If they were late, a fine was deducted from their measly wages. Many children became ill or fell asleep at work, which increased the risk of accidents.

A Spinning Mule at Trowbridge Museum

Exhausted children were often hit with a strap or had their heads dipped in water. One hospital reported that in one year it treated 1,000 children who had been hurt at work. One of the most dangerous jobs was picking up the bits of cloth that dropped from the weaving machines. This was called "scavenging". What's worse is that the children had to "scavenge" while the machines were working so that production didn't halt and the factory owners made more money.

This Way!

Colour in the white outline of the poor child "scavenging" under the machine.

# Try this Trowbridge crossword

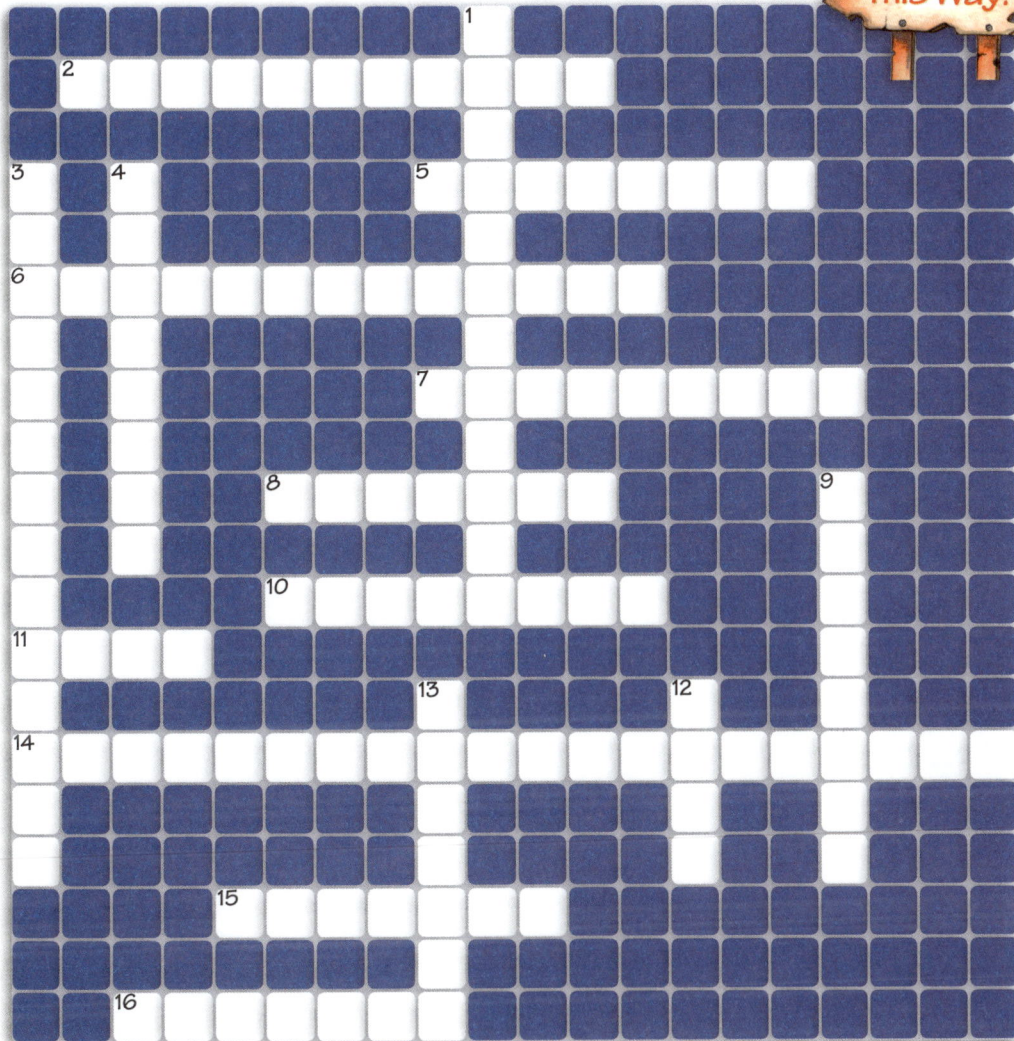

**This Way!**

## Clues Across

2. Frame on which cloth is stretched (11)
5. Person who controls cloth production (8)
6. Spinning machine with several spindles (8,5)
7. Person who collects bits of cloth (9)
8. Building where goods are produced (7)
10. Person who looks after sheep (8)
11. A fossil fuel (4)
14. Great change from production by hand to production by machines (10,10)
15. Making a fabric through interlacing thread (7)
16. Shrinking and thickening cloth (7)

## Clues Down

1. The fabric that made Trowbridge rich (7,5)
3. Manufacture of a large number of goods (4,10)
4. Drawing out wool into a long thread (8)
9. Woman who spins thread (8)
12. A machine for weaving yarn (4)
13. Process by which wool is straightened and cleaned (7)

Answers on page 32

The only education for children who worked in the factories was Sunday school. The first Sunday school in Trowbridge was at the Tabernacle church, where you learnt to read and write by studying the Bible. Imagine working 14 hours a day and then going to school on a Sunday! Would you be able to concentrate?

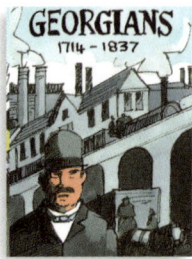

# A FACTORY INVESTIGATION

In 1833 a Factories Inquiry Commission was set up by the government. Below is an extract from the list provided by J & T Clark of Trowbridge of the people employed in their mill in Duke Street. The list shows that in the three mills owned by J & T Clark a total of 99 people were employed. Of these, 45 were aged 15 or under; 11 of these were aged 10 or 11. So 45% (nearly half) of the employees were children.

- 20/- (£1) would have been worth roughly £100 today.

- Of the 99 employees only two had "No" in the "Healthy" column. One 12-year-old boy was said to suffer from **rheumatism** and a 14-year-old boy to have "occasional headaches".

- Why did the mill owners want to employ so many children? (Look at the wages column in the table below.)

- How would the parents have felt about their children working in the mills? (Remember most families were very poor. Children had been expected to start working at an early age long before factories came along. It was considered "normal" then.)

| | AGE | Number of children | Of whom living | Dead | No. of years employed | Daily work hrs Mon-Fri | +Hours worked Saturday | Weekly wage | Can read? | Can write? | Healthy? |
|---|---|---|---|---|---|---|---|---|---|---|---|
| George Sheppherd | 36 | 8 | 4 | 4 | 1 | 12 | 6 | 20/- | Yes | No | Yes |
| James Reynolds | 11 | - | - | - | 1 | 12 | 6 | 2/6d | Yes | No | Yes |
| Sarah Reynolds | 12 | | | - | 5 mnths | 12 | 6 | 2/6d | Yes | No | Yes |
| Mary Ann Martin | 15 | - | - | - | 7 | 12 | 6 | 2/6d | Yes | No | Yes |
| Sarah Martin | 10 | - | - | - | 3 mnths | 12 | 6 | 2/6d | Yes | No | Yes |
| Matilda Martin | 12 | - | - | - | 5 mnths | 12 | 6 | 2/6d | Yes | No | Yes |
| Henry Townsend | 10 | - | - | - | 2 | 12 | 6 | 2/6d | Yes | No | Yes |
| Edward Cox | 10 | - | - | - | 3 | 12 | 6 | 2/6d | Yes | No | Yes |
| Ben Rose | 40 | 6 | 4 | 2 | 14 | 13 | 6 | 16/- | Yes | No | Yes |

## Examine the evidence

This Way!

Imagine that you were a member of the Commission investigating the Clarks' mills. Using evidence from the table opposite and other information, consider the following statements and mark **T** for true and **F** for false:

1  No children under 10 were employed ☐

2  Young children had to work long hours ☐

3  Children were paid good wages ☐

4  Standards of education were very high at that time ☐

5  Children from the same family often worked in the same factory ☐

6  Nearly everyone working in these mills was very healthy. (Think carefully. Can we trust the information in the list?) ☐

Answers on page 32

## Where do people in Trowbridge work today?

No single business dominates the town as the woollen industry once did. The largest employers today are Virgin Mobile Telecoms and Wiltshire County Council, whose offices are in Bythesea Road.

## The decline of the woollen industry

Towards the end of the 19th century the woollen industry in Trowbridge began to decline in the face of competition from other parts of the country – notably Yorkshire and Scotland. In 1982 Salters (who had taken over J & T Clark) was the last mill to close.

In 1833 a Factory Act was passed, which changed the working conditions of children:

- Children under 9 could no longer be employed at all.

- Children from 9 to 13 could be employed for a maximum of 8 hours per day.

- Children from 13 to 18 could be employed for 12 hours per day.

*County Hall in 1950*

# THOMAS HELLIKER,

At the end of the 1700s, the new power-driven machines were not welcomed by everyone. Workers in the woollen cloth industry worried that these machines would do them out of their jobs. And if you lost your job, you and your family could starve. Many workers tried to stop mill owners using the new machines.

In Trowbridge, in the summer of 1802, three mills were burned down and large numbers of soldiers were sent to the town to keep order. Rewards were offered to encourage people to give information about the mill burners.

Thomas Helliker, a young cloth worker from Trowbridge, was publicly hanged in Salisbury on March 22nd, 1803 – the day of his 19th birthday. Was he an innocent youth who died protecting others – or did he deserve to die? Consider the evidence and make your own decision.

Francis Naish was one Trowbridge clothier who was determined to introduce the new machinery. His main workshops were in the Conigre in Trowbridge, but he also owned a fulling mill at Littleton near Semington. He let this to another clothier called Ralph Heath.

By July 1802 Heath was so afraid of his mill being attacked that he and 3 of his workmen stayed on watch every night in Heath's cottage next door to the mill. They took turns patrolling the mill. However, at 1.00am on July 23rd, armed men, some with blackened faces, burst in to the cottage. Heath claimed one man held them at gunpoint, threatening to "...blow out their brains if anyone offered to move" while the others left to start a fire. Littleton Mill was burned to the ground.

# HERO OR VILLAIN?

Thomas Helliker was an eighteen-year-old apprentice at Naish's workshop in Trowbridge. On August 3rd Naish declared to the local magistrates that he was convinced Helliker was involved in the burning of Littleton Mill. Helliker was arrested and locked up. Two days later Ralph Heath identified Helliker as the man who had held them at gunpoint in the cottage.

Thomas Helliker was imprisoned in Salisbury. At his trial he was found guilty and was hanged on March 22nd 1803. Friends and workmates were among the crowd that watched the execution. He maintained his innocence throughout but refused to accuse anyone else of the crime.

Public executions were a popular spectator sport in England. In this illustration the convicted criminal is taken to Salisbury market square on the back of a horse-drawn cart. The noose is placed around his neck and then the horse is moved on so the man falls and the noose jerks tight.

# THOMAS HELLIKER,

This Way!

What evidence is there to support the view that Thomas Helliker was guilty?

What evidence is there to support the view that he was innocent?

## GUILTY

## NOT GUILTY

**WHAT IS YOUR VERDICT – GUILTY OR NOT GUILTY? TICK A BOX!**

### RALPH HEATH

His **testimony** was the key reason for Helliker's **conviction**. He identified Helliker as the man who held them at gunpoint while the mill was set alight. Heath received a reward of £500 for the information he had given. Under **cross-examination** he said that Helliker's face had not been so black as to be unrecognisable. He also said that at one time he had claimed not to recognise Helliker but this was because he feared "his life was in danger".

### JOHN PEARCE

Pearce was one of the 3 men helping Heath to watch over the mill on the night of the fire. In his statement he said: "Mr Heath never looked up the whole time but kept looking to the ground." Pearce also said that the only man to carry a pistol was a "short" man - a description that did not match Helliker. Neither Pearce nor the other two of Heath's workmen on watch that fateful night were asked to give evidence at the trial.

### JOSEPH WARREN

Warren and Helliker were great friends. They were both apprentices at the Conigre workshop. On the day Helliker was arrested, Warren went to the magistrates and swore a statement. He claimed he had met Helliker in Trowbridge outside a friend's house at 10.30pm on the night of the fire. He said Helliker was drunk so they both slept in the friend's kitchen all night until 5am when Helliker left for work. The following morning Warren disappeared and turned up in Leeds in September. Warren never appeared at the trial.

### THOMAS HELLIKER

Would the men who planned the attack on Littleton Mill have allowed such a young man – a mere apprentice – to have been so heavily involved? This young man spent almost 8 lonely months in prison before his final execution. He claimed throughout that he was innocent. Naming others may have brought him a reduced sentence – perhaps **transportation** to a prison colony in Australia – but he never did. After the execution, the body of Thomas Helliker was placed in a hearse and brought back across Salisbury Plain to Trowbridge. A large crowd accompanied the body to the Parish church of St James where he was finally laid to rest.

# GUILTY OR NOT GUILTY?

The tomb of Thomas Helliker can still be seen in the graveyard at St James' Church.
Go to see it and read the inscription on it.

*The Parish Church of St James in about 1955*

A newspaper article published soon after the execution ended with the comment:

*"… a severe example was necessary to restore a due reverence (which means respect) for the law."*

Was this the real reason for his execution? To frighten others into obeying the law?

# A VOICE FOR THE PEOPLE

Some people say that when you want something to change, you've got to go straight to the top and this is what the Chartists tried to do in the 19th century. The Chartists were so called because they drew up a list of 6 aims in a document they called the "People's Charter". Their objective was to reform the way Britain was governed. Laws were made in Parliament as they are today. Parliament is where the individuals we elect to represent us – called Members of Parliament and MPs for short – meet to discuss these laws. When the laws are passed they are called Acts of Parliament. Nowadays everyone in Britain who is 18 years or older is entitled to vote for an MP to represent them in an **election**.

But 200 years ago many men were not allowed to vote and no women were at all! The people who ruled the country didn't consider women capable of choosing an MP or even of knowing what was best for them. An Act of Parliament passed in 1832 went some way to improving the political system, but many people thought it did not go nearly far enough. For example, the right to vote was only given to men who owned property. So working men – many of whom were suffering extreme hardship, often as a result of the Industrial Revolution – were ruled out. Two types of worker were affected:

a) People who worked from home such as the hand-loom weavers. They were in danger of losing their jobs because of mass-production in factories.

b) Factory workers. When there was a big demand for the goods made in factories, such as cloth, jobs were plentiful, but if production decreased, then workers could be laid off at the drop of a hat.

---

The aims of the "People's Charter" were:

1. A vote for every man (not woman!) over 21. ☐

2. Voting should be done by secret ballot. ☐

3. Any man should be allowed to stand for Parliament, not just people who owned property. ☐

4. All MPs should be paid. This would mean that not only rich people could stand for election. ☐

5. All **constituencies** that send a representative to Parliament must be of equal size. ☐

6. Elections for Parliament should take place every year. ☐

Find out which of these aims were eventually achieved and put a tick next to them.

---

**This Way!**

Write down 3 aims that you think, if achieved, could improve life in your town.

☐

☐

☐

# The Courts

*The Courts, Holt*

**This Way!**

The first Chartist meeting in the area was in the nearby village of Holt. Go and visit the beautiful gardens at The Courts, owned by the National Trust. These gardens were once the site of a mill that produced woollen cloth. Think about why a mill was built here. Clue: find the water features in the garden. The house was once owned by a rich clothier.

*The Courts garden, Holt*

Soldiers were sent to Trowbridge to keep order at Chartist meetings and prevent violence. But the machines stopped working when the factory workers walked out and children locked out their schoolmaster and joined the protest.

*Chartists meeting at night outside Sadlers Mill*

When the First World War broke out in 1914, hundreds of Trowbridge men answered the call to serve their "King and Country". Over 300 never returned and their names are recorded on the war memorial inside the entrance to Trowbridge Park.

Less than 20 years later, England was at war again and the memorial also honours the names of those who died in the Second World War. Go to the memorial and study the list of names. Do you recognise any of the surnames?

**This Way!**

*This photo of County Hall was taken in 1950, five years after the end of the Second World War.*

During the Second World War, many cities were bombed from the air in what were called air-raids. In Trowbridge a huge **camouflage** net was put over the County Hall building.

*This photo was taken in 1923, five years after the end of the First World War.*

Trowbridge was not greatly affected by air-raids, but there was a tragic incident in 1942 when three bombs fell near the Town Bridge, killing two teenage girls. Why do you think these three stray bombs were dropped on Trowbridge? Clue: Bath and Bristol suffered frequent air raids. Look at a map to see how close those cities are to Trowbridge. Another blast also took the roof off the Blind House.

Go to the Blind House and read the information plaque beside it. What was it used for? Why was it called the "Blind House"?

a. Because it was a home for people who couldn't see.

b. Because it was a place where "blind drunk" people could sober up.

c. Because it didn't have any windows.

Answer on page 32.

This Way!

# Far from home

During the Second World War, children were evacuated from their homes in London and other cities, which were being bombed. Many **evacuees** came to Trowbridge to stay with host families who cared for them until it was safe to return to the cities.

People from Trowbridge are nicknamed "knobs" because of the stone sphere on top of the Blind House.

**This Way!** Read "Goodnight Mr Tom" by Michelle Magorian. It's a brilliant book about an evacuee.

# The Spitfire Legend

Weapons and equipment for the armed forces were made in the Haden factory in Silver Street. Parts for Spitfire aircraft were made in factories in Hilperton Road and Bradley Road. England had not been invaded since 1066, when William the Conqueror defeated King Harold at the Battle of Hastings. In the Second World War, Hitler wanted to invade Great Britain and in the summer of 1940 German aeroplanes began their attack. The fighting between the German and British airforces was called the Battle of Britain. The Germans were defeated and the Spitfire achieved legendary status.

Find out more about the Spitfire and the Battle of Britain at www.Battle-of-Britain.com

The Spitfire was designed by Reginald Joseph Mitchell.

It was called Spitfire because that was a word for a fiery-tempered lady.

The Spitfire was the fastest British fighter plane – faster than the Hurricane.

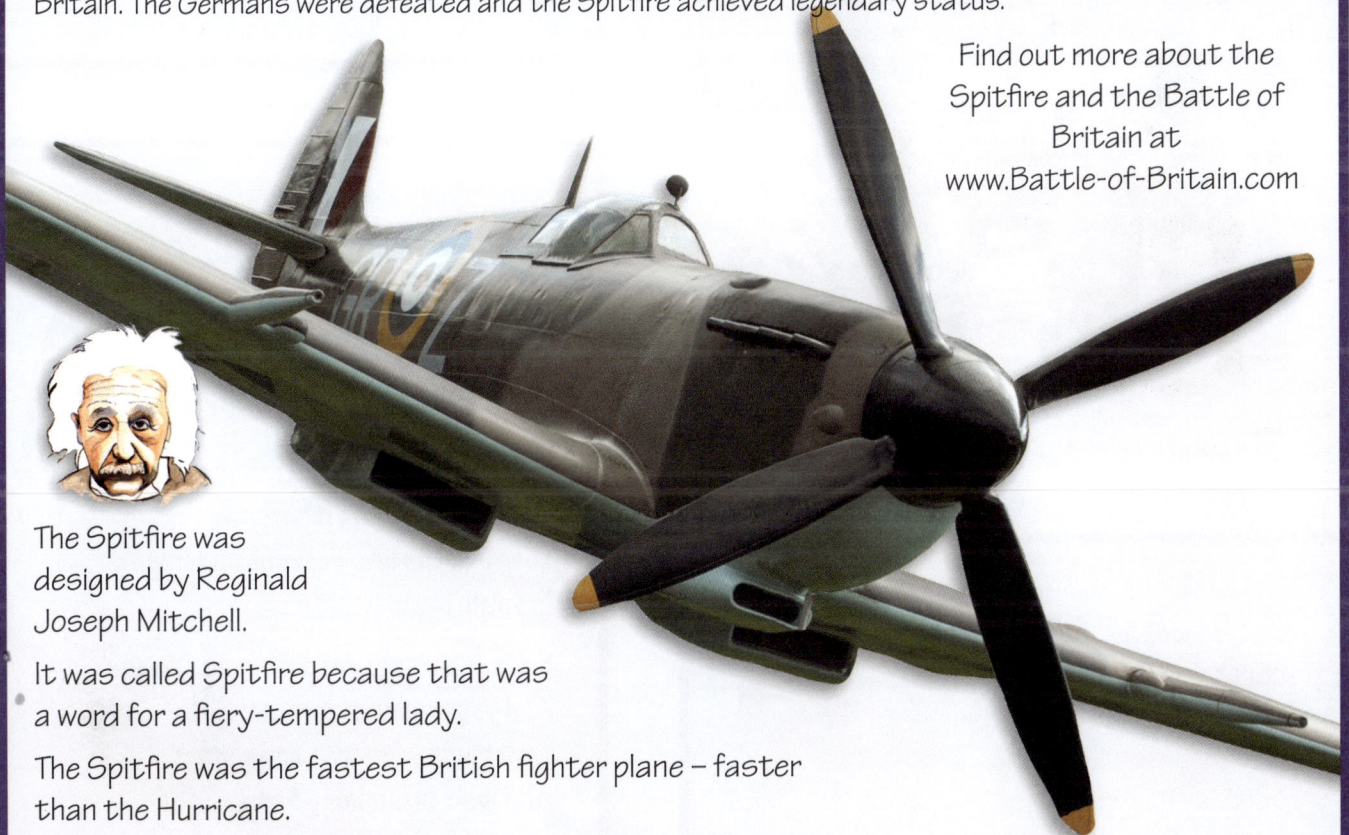

# TROWBRIDGE CELEBRITIES

## George Crabbe

George Crabbe came to Trowbridge in 1814, when he was 60, to be **rector** of St James' parish church. He started his career as a doctor, but what he is remembered for is his poetry. At that time many poems were about country life, portraying it as beautiful and happy, particularly when compared with life in the new industrial towns. But George Crabbe wanted to show in his poems that this was not true and many poor people suffered severe hardship in the countryside.

Read these lines from his poem, *The Village*:

I grant indeed that fields and flocks have charms
For him that grazes or for him that farms;
But when amid such pleasing scenes I trace
The poor laborious natives of the place,
And see the mid-day sun, with fervid ray,
On their bare heads and dewy temples play;...
Then shall I dare these real ills to hide...?

**This Way!** How do you think life in the country compares with life in a town today? Try and write a poem that expresses your thoughts. George Crabbe's poem uses rhyme, but yours doesn't have to.

• Another of his poems was used as the basis for a famous opera called *Peter Grimes* by the **composer**, Benjamin Britten.

When Crabbe died many more poems were discovered that had not been published in his lifetime.
In *The Comparison* he compares friendship and love.
What are the differences?

Friendship is like gold refined
And all may weigh its worth;
Love like the ore, brought undesign'd
In virgin beauty forth.

Friendship may pass from age to age,
And yet remain the same;
Love must in many a toil engage,
And melt in lambent flame.

**This Way!** Go and read the memorial to George Crabbe on the north wall of the chancel in St James' Church. It says that he wasn't born rich, but he was successful because of his genius.

# Sir Isaac Pitman

Sir Isaac Pitman's fame was also to do with words! He invented a very quick way of writing called shorthand, even quicker than text messaging. His system was phonetic. That means it was based on the sounds of words, which were written down with simple pencil strokes. He introduced it in 1837, the same year that Queen Victoria ascended the throne. These days people who work in offices use computers for word-processing, but a generation ago, letters were dictated to secretaries who wrote in a shorthand notebook and then typed out the letters on a typewriter.

Shorthand

**ur my best m8**

Text message

**You are my best mate.**

Standard English

Go and find Isaac Pitman's memorial plaque on the Town Hall.
This photo shows the Town Hall and old market place in about 1955.
What can you see today that is different?
Write two differences, **1.** in standard spelling and **2.** in text message spelling.

1.

2.

## THE FATHER OF PHOTOGRAPHY
### William Henry Fox Talbot

Fox Talbot is often called the 'father of photography'. But he was not the first person to capture an image and print it, because Louis Daguerre, a Frenchman, had invented 'daguerrotypes' in 1837. The trouble was that you couldn't make copies of them: if you wanted another one, the photographer had to take the shot again – which was good for business if you were a photographer!

*Photograph of a portrait of Fox Talbot at Lacock, taken around 1955 by a Frith photographer*

So the 'Holy Grail', if photography was to develop as a business and an art form, was to find a way of copying photographs. The peaceful 13th-century nunnery at Lacock, where Fox Talbot lived, seems an unlikely place for the Grail to have been found. But during the 1830s and early 1840s he toiled away with papers and chemicals, while trying to use a camera very different from the ones we use today; it was a simple wooden box that his wife called 'Henry's little mousetrap'.

He produced the world's first photographic negative in 1835: a blurred view, in reverse, of a window at the abbey. He followed this up in 1840 with the first 'calotype' – *kalos* means 'beautiful' in Greek – a type of photographic print made by washing bromine paper in gallic acid and silver salts. Calotypes cost a fraction of the price of daguerrotypes to produce and took far less time. So Fox Talbot's daughters sent their friends pictures of themselves – copies of the original photograph. Not quite as simple as photo-messaging!

Lacock Abbey and its grounds, set beside the beautiful village of Lacock, are all in the care of The National Trust and open to visitors. You can see Fox Talbot's amazing work in the museum of photography there.

You can also see his wonderful plants in the botanical gardens. The interior of the medieval Lacock Abbey was used as the classroom of Hogwarts school in the Harry Potter films, where Harry would sit with his fellow wizard apprentices.

*Lacock Abbey in 1904*

These calotypes were not an overnight success, for Talbot had other interests that took up his time – he was a politician, mathematician, painter and astronomer, and had a life-long interest in translating ancient Assyrian inscriptions. Eventually, he gave the job of making calotyping a commercial enterprise to his valet, Nicolas Henneman. They set up a printing works in Reading, but this too was not a success.

# PHOTOGRAPHERS

## Francis Frith

Francis Frith, whose company took most of the photographs in this book, was a very different kettle of fish from Fox Talbot. He was the son of a barrel maker, and made his fortune in the grocery business in Liverpool. He retired a millionaire at the age of 34, determined to pursue his passion for photography.

Endlessly energetic, Frith travelled to Egypt in 1857, journeying down the Nile with his heavy brass cameras. The conditions for picture taking confound belief. Frith laboured for hours in his wicker dark room in the sweltering desert heat, while the volatile chemicals fizzed dangerously in their trays. He was held captive by bandits and attacked by wild dogs.

Unlike Fox Talbot, Frith was a good businessman, and on his return to England immediately set up a photographic company; his aim was to photograph every town and village in Britain. Travelling by train and pony and trap, Frith took thousands of photos of towns, villages, seaside resorts and beauty spots that were keenly bought by millions of Victorian tourists as souvenirs. By 1890 he had created the greatest photographic company of its kind in the world.

Exposure times for calotypes could be as long as two hours, but by the 1850s they were down to two minutes. Early photographs show sitters leaning against walls or chairs to stay still. Photographers also used a metal neck brace, cunningly kept out of sight behind the sitter's head.

This Way!

**This Way!**

**Plot yourself a Trowbridge walkabout**

Here are ten photographs of some of Trowbridge's best-loved landmarks. Draw an arrow from each photograph to its location on this Ordnance Survey map (drawn in 1922). Then draw a dotted line on the map, to plot yourself a walk around Trowbridge, taking in as many of the landmarks as you can.

1. Town Hall 1900

2. Holy Trinity Church 1900

3. Fore Street 1900

4. Silver Street 1900

5. Fore Street 1900

6. Wingfield Road 1907

7. The Park Lake c1955

8. Roundstone Street c1955

# KNOW YOUR TOWN?

How have these places changed since the photographs were taken?

1
2
3
4
5
6
7
8
9
10

9 Bradford Road 1907

10 The Girls' High School c1965

# TROWBRIDGE QUIZ

**1** Trowbridge comes from a Saxon word meaning what?
a) Town bridge
b) Tall bridge
c) Tree bridge
d) True brick
check out page 4.

**2** Who ordered the survey known as the Domesday Book?
a) Brictric the Saxon
b) William the Conqueror
c) King Harold
d) Humphrey de Bohun
check out page 5.

**3** Who laid siege to Trowbridge Castle?
a) King Stephen
b) Henry VIII
c) Thomas Hungerford
d) Thomas the Tank
check out pagse 6 and 7.

**4** Which important industry grew during the Middle Ages?
a) Coal mining
b) Wine
c) Weapons
d) Woollen cloth
check out  pages 8 and 9.

**5** What speeded up spinning in the 18th century?
a) Spinning Julie
b) Spinsters
c) Spinning Jenny
d) Sleeping Beauty
check out pages 10 and 11.

**6** How many children of 10 or 11 were employed in the mills of J & T Clark in 1833?
a) 7
b) 11
c) 19
d) 25
check out pages 14 and 15.

**7** Which local mill was attacked and burned down on July 23rd 1802?
a) Littleton Mill
b) Ashton Mill
c) Bridge Mill
d) Courts Mill
check out pages 16 and 17.

**8** Which building was covered by a huge net during the Second World War?
a) The Town Hall
b) Holy Trinity Church
c) Asda
d) County Hall
check out pages 22 and 23.

**9** Which well known poet was once rector of St James' Church?
a) William Wordsworth
b) George Crabbe
c) William Shakespeare
d) Harry Potter
check out pages 24.

**10** Who were pioneering photographers?
a) William Henry Fox Talbot
b) Harry Potter
c) William the Conqueror
d) Francis Frith
check out pages 26 and 27.

# GLOSSARY AND FURTHER INFORMATION

**Botanist -** someone who studies plants..

**Bronze Age -** the name given to the period in the past when people began to make things out of bronze as well as stone.

**Camouflage -** a means of disguising someone or something to fit in with its surroundings.

**Chamber Pot –** a pot for urine used in bedrooms.

**Civil War –** a war fought between people of the same country.

**Clothiers -** people whose business is manufacturing cloth or clothes.

**Composer -** a person who creates a musical work.

**Constituencies -** the name for an area and the people who live there who elect an MP to represent them.

**Conviction -** when someone is found guilty of a crime.

**Cross-examination -** when a witness in a trial is asked questions.

**Daguerrotype -** an early type of photograph.

**Economy -** the management of resources in the community, taking into account how well off people are and the services that are available to them.

**Election -** when a person is chosen by vote.

**Evacuees -** people sent away from a place of danger in wartime. People were sent away from their homes in the cities that were being bombed in the Second World War.

**Inhabitants -** the people living in a particular area.

**Mass- production -** when a large number of goods are produced on a large scale, mainly using machines.

**Medieval -** the adjective that describes things relating to the Middle Ages.

**Norman Conquest –** This happened in 1066 when William, Duke of Normandy (in France) defeated King Harold at the Battle of Hastings and conquered England.

**Rector –** a minister of the Church of England.

**Rheumatism -** painful disorder of the joints and muscles.

**Siege –** when a castle is surrounded by an enemy who tries to defeat the people within by cutting off their supplies.

**Testimony -** evidence given in a trial.

**Transportation -** A punishment that forces people to leave their homes and transports them to another country, often Australia.

## FURTHER INFORMATION

Trowbridge Museum, The Shires, Court Street, Trowbridge BA14 8AT.
www.nationaltrust.org.uk/learninganddiscovery   www.wessexarch.co.uk/learning
**Some good history web sites:**
www.eyewitnesstohistory.com    www.historylearningsite.co.uk    www.schoolhistory.co.uk
www.bbc.co.uk/history   www.swgfl.org.uk/learning
**Two brilliant books:**
Trowbridge: A History and Celebration by Dee la Vardera.
Trowbridge: History and Guide by Kenneth Rogers.

# TROWBRIDGE ANSWERS

## HERE ARE THE ANSWERS TO THE MOTTE AND BAILEY WORDMATCH ON PAGE 7:

1. WOODEN KEEP
2. MOTTE
3. BAILEY
4. MOAT
5. GATEWAY
6. PALLISADE

## HERE ARE THE ANSWERS TO THE CROSSWORD ON PAGE 13:

Across:
2. TENTERHOOKS
5. CLOTHIER
6. SPINNING JENNY
7. SCAVENGER
8. FACTORY
10. SHEPHERD
11. COAL
14. INDUSTRIAL REVOLUTION
15. WEAVING
16. FULLING

Down:
1. WOOLLEN CLOTH
3. MASS PRODUCTION
4. SPINNING
9. SPINSTER
12. LOOM
13. CARDING

## ANSWERS TO EXAMINE THE EVIDENCE ON PAGE 15:

1-F 2-T 3-F 4-F 5-T 6-F

## ANSWER TO BLIND HOUSE ON PAGE 23: C

## ANSWERS TO WALKABOUT ON PAGE 29:

A-2 B-5 C-6 D-4 E-1 F-3 G-7 H-9 I-8 J-10

## ANSWERS TO QUIZ ON PAGE 30:

1 - c) Tree bridge  2 - b) William the Conqueror  3 - a) King Stephen
4 - d) Woollen cloth  5 - c) Spinning Jenny  6 - b) 11  7 - a) Littleton Mill  8 - d) County Hall
9 - b) George Crabbe  10 - a) William Henry Fox Talbot and d) Francis Frith

## FIND FRANCIS – Where was he lurking?

Page 6 - Wicker Hill
Page 9 - Fore Street
Page 19 - St James' Church
Page 22 - The War Memorial

Project Editor Emma Worth.  Designed by Julian Hight.  Illustrations by David Mostyn, Shelley Tolcher & Julie Brockway.
Photographs copyright © The Francis Frith Collection www.francisfrith.com  Additional photographs by Julian Hight.
British Library Cataloguing in Publication Data
Paperback edition: ISBN 10: 1-906112-00-2  ISBN 13: 978-1-906112-00-4
Hardback edition: ISBN 10: 1-906112-01-0  ISBN 13: 978-1-906112-01-1

Explore Trowbridge by John Collingwood and Emma Worth.

Published by Heritage Content Company Ltd, Frith's Barn, Teffont, Salisbury, Wiltshire SP3 5QP  Tel: +44 (0) 1722 717 138
Printed and bound in Malaysia